PERSPECTIVES ON THE
INDUSTRIAL REVOLUTION

by Carla Mooney

12 STORY LIBRARY

www.12StoryLibrary.com

12-Story Library is an imprint of Bookstaves and Press Room Editions

Produced for 12-Story Library by Red Line Editorial

Photographs ©: A.P. Tates/Library of Congress, cover, 1; David Wilson CC2.0, 5, 11; ullstein bild/Getty Images, 4, 18–19; National Photo Company Collection/Library of Congress, 6; Oleg Znamenskiy/Shutterstock Images, 7; North Wind Picture Archives, 8, 10; oYOo/Shutterstock Images, 9; Everett Historical/Shutterstock Images, 12, 25; Detroit Publishing Company/Library of Congress, 13; Library of Congress, 14, 28; H. W. Phillips/Library of Congress, 15; Bain News Service/George Grantham Bain Collection/Library of Congress, 16, 22; Sean Pavone/Shutterstock Images, 17; Lewis Wickes Hine/Library of Congress, 20; Harris & Ewing Collection/Library of Congress, 21; M. Spencer Green/AP Images, 23; Johnston (Frances Benjamin) Collection/Library of Congress, 26; Gordon Bell/Shutterstock Images, 27; Benjamin Beytekin/picture-alliance/dpa/AP Images, 29

Content Consultant: Martin J. Hershock, Dean of College of Arts, Sciences, and Letters and Professor of History, University of Michigan–Dearborn

Library of Congress Cataloging-in-Publication Data
A catalog record for this book is available from the Library of Congress
978-1-63235-402-0 (hardcover)
978-1-63235-474-7 (paperback)
978-1-62143-526-6 (ebook)

Printed in the United States of America
022017

Access free, up-to-date content on this topic plus a full digital version of this book. Scan the QR code on page 31 or use your school's login at 12StoryLibrary.com.

Table of Contents

Fact Sheet

What was the Industrial Revolution?

Many inventions and innovations were created during the Industrial Revolution. Machines started doing the work of people. New sources of power were developed. New processes made manufacturers more efficient. These changes helped people make goods faster and more cheaply. This made life easier for some people. For others, the Industrial Revolution forever changed the way they were able to make a living. As machines took their jobs, many had no choice but to work in factories.

When did the Industrial Revolution happen?

The Industrial Revolution began in the late 1700s in Great Britain. It spread to the rest of Europe and the United States. The revolution happened in two parts. Most industrialization happened in the United States during the second part. During this time period, more people used science to figure out how and why inventions worked. But historians don't agree on exactly when the first revolution ended and the second began. Historians also disagree on when the second revolution ended. Some say as early

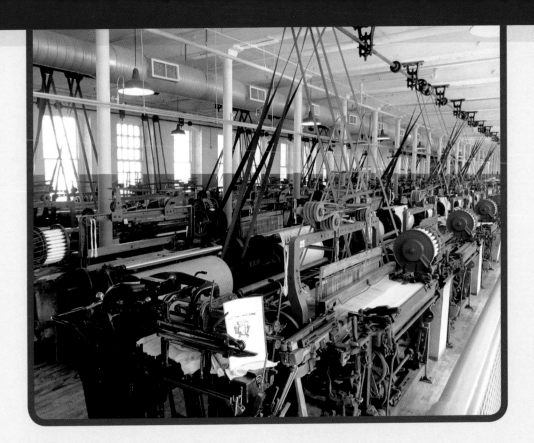

as 1914. Others say it was still going on in the 1930s.

How did the Industrial Revolution change the world?

Factories full of machines were built in towns and cities. Many people moved from farms into cities to look for work in factories as their old jobs disappeared. Labor unions emerged to protect the rights of workers and to fight for better pay and working conditions.

One of the biggest advances of the Industrial Revolution was the improvement of the steam engine. Steam engines powered machines, railroads, steamships, and more. The telegraph was also invented during this time. It made communicating across large distances easier and faster. Messages could be sent and received in minutes. And transportation became easier with the building of railroads and steamships and the invention of the automobile.

Cotton Gin Permanently Changes the South

In the 1700s, growing and selling cotton was a difficult chore. Cotton has tiny green seeds that workers had to remove by hand. The process was long and hard. Farmers made little money selling cotton since it took so long to pick out the seeds.

Inventor Eli Whitney worked on a machine to make picking the seeds out of cotton easier. In 1793, Whitney finished his cotton gin. The gin was a machine that combed out the cotton's green seeds. What once took several workers an entire day, the cotton gin could do in one hour. Farmers quickly realized that Whitney's gin could make them very rich. They planted entire fields with

PATENTS

Eli Whitney's cotton gin had a deep impact on agriculture in the South. But he did not become the rich inventor he thought he would. Whitney patented his invention in 1794. That meant no one else could legally make a cotton gin like Whitney's. But farmers and plantation owners started to make copies of his cotton gin. Whitney and his business partner tried to stop these illegal versions. They spent a lot of time filing lawsuits but saw little money.

Eli Whitney's cotton gin

1794
Year Eli Whitney received a patent for his cotton gin.

- The cotton gin reduced the amount of time needed to pick the seeds from cotton.
- Because of the cotton gin, southern farmers planted more cotton and became the world's largest producer of cotton in the 1800s.
- Southern landowners relied on slavery instead of paying workers.
- Free black people were kidnapped and sold as slaves in the South to work on cotton plantations.

cotton. Soon, farms across the southern United States grew cotton. They quickly became the global leader in cotton production. The cotton gin brought those who owned farmland new riches and prosperity.

But farmers still needed people to plant and harvest all that cotton. Rather than pay workers, many landowners became slaveholders instead. The number of enslaved people in the United States significantly increased in the first half of the 1800s. Many southern landowners began to think slavery was necessary to their way of life.

For black people in the United States, the cotton gin was not progress. Those who were free and living in the South had to wear an identification tag or risk being sold as a slave. Some free black people living in northern states were kidnapped. They were then sold into slavery to pick cotton in the South. Many historians think the invention of the cotton gin was one reason for the US Civil War.

7

Factory Workers Face Difficult Conditions

During the Industrial Revolution, many people took factory jobs. Some simply hoped for a better life. Others had no choice, as machines took over the work they used to do. They all quickly discovered that factories were grim places to work. A factory worker typically had to work 12 to 16 hours a day. In the winter, factories were very cold because they did not have heat. In the summer, factories were very hot and humid. The steam engines made it worse. And the work itself was usually boring for workers, since they had to repeat the same task all day long.

Life as a factory worker was also dangerous. Factories had few windows for fresh air, so pollution filled the buildings. Poor lighting led to many accidents. Machines without safety devices crushed workers' hands and arms. Some experienced even worse injuries. Metalworkers handled toxic materials every day and faced dangers from burns and explosions.

A drawing of iron factory workers in the mid-1800s

8

For many people, these poor working conditions led to health problems. Fabric workers developed lung diseases from breathing cotton dust and fibers. Workers who got hurt or sick had to find their own way to the hospital or doctor. They often didn't have enough money to pay for medicine. Workers were not paid while they healed. If they stayed home to recover, other workers might take their job.

Today's factory workers have protective gear to keep them safer.

10

Percentage of men who were killed or injured each year in one Chicago steel factory near the end of the Industrial Revolution.

- Factory workers often labored 12 to 16 hours per day.
- Conditions in factories were difficult and dangerous, often leading to injury and illness.
- Workers had to pay their own medical bills and could be fired for staying home to heal.

THINK ABOUT IT

How were owners able to get workers for their factories in spite of the poor conditions? Why do you think people continued to work in factories? Why didn't workers leave for better jobs?

Mill Girls of Lowell Work Long Days

Lowell, Massachusetts, was the United States' first factory town. Many of the factories were textile mills, which turned raw cotton into woven fabric. Most of the first workers in the Lowell mills were young women. The women were usually between 15 and 25 years old. They left their family farms. Some of the help they used to provide on the farms was now done by machines. Many looked for new opportunities in the city. In the 1800s and early 1900s, women had few rights. They couldn't vote. They couldn't own property. The mills opened up a new world of options for these women. They could earn their own money and spend it how they wanted. Women working at the mill usually earned between $1.85 and $3.00 per week, about half the wage of a man.

But mill work was long and hard. The women worked 12- to 14-hour

More than 8,000 people worked in the Lowell mills in 1840.

Lowell textile mills

days in the factories. They worked on large machines that quickly turned cotton into thread. Most of the mill girls lived in large buildings called boardinghouses. A typical boardinghouse held 20 to 40 women. Usually, each girl shared a bedroom with three other women. The women had to be back at the boardinghouse by a certain time each night. They signed contracts promising to attend church on Sundays and follow other rules of conduct.

The women became friends with one another. They ate together in the boardinghouse dining room. They wrote letters, sewed, and played the piano. They were able to visit libraries and read books not available back home. Life in the city offered mill girls the chance to learn and try new things.

2 million

Amount of cloth, in yards (1.8 million m), Lowell textile mills produced in one week by 1855.

- Women typically earned $1.85 to $3.00 per week working in the Lowell mills.
- The average workday for a mill girl was 12 to 14 hours long.
- Women stayed at boardinghouses and formed friendships with one another.

11

Urban Slums Are Overcrowded

During the Industrial Revolution, many people who lived on farms thought life in a city might be better. Some could no longer make a living as machines took over work in the fields. They heard news of factory jobs and moved away from the country into cities. Those cities grew quickly. But many cities weren't prepared for the steady stream of new workers. New people often had a hard time finding a decent place to live. Many poor workers ended up living in city slums. Some were required to live there because of the color of their skin.

New York City apartment in 1910

DEADLY TUBERCULOSIS

Tuberculosis was one of the deadliest diseases in industrial cities during this time period. The disease is an infection that attacks a person's lungs. It spreads through the air. The disease was easy to catch in the overcrowded urban slums. During the Industrial Revolution, there was no cure for the disease.

4,300

People who died of bronchitis and pneumonia in Chicago in 1891.

- Factory work drew many people to cities, especially those that had lost their jobs working in the fields.
- Many poor workers crowded into cheaply made housing.
- Outbreaks of sickness and disease killed thousands of people living in cities.

Immigrants crowded into the Lower East Side of New York City in the early 1900s.

Many people crowded into small houses and tiny apartments. Sometimes an entire family lived in a single room. One famous slum in New York City was called Five Points. Some apartments there had ceilings that were so low occupants couldn't stand up straight. Many children had to sleep on piles of rags on the floor. Buildings in slums did not have indoor plumbing. Everyone shared an outdoor toilet. For cooking and cleaning, residents carried in water from outside, sometimes up several flights of stairs. Often this water was polluted.

It was hard for factory workers who lived in these crowded buildings to stay healthy. The streets they lived on were filled with litter and horse manure. Mice, rats, and fleas contaminated their homes. Many developed breathing and lung problems. Cholera, tuberculosis, and smallpox spread easily from person to person. Diseases killed many of those who moved to cities with dreams of a better life.

13

The Industrial Revolution helped the American middle classes grow. Before the Industrial Revolution, most of society in cities was divided into two main classes. A small number of people belonged to the upper class. They did not have to work and were born into wealth and privilege. Many more people were part of the working class. They had little money. Some people were in the middle. They were first called the middle classes after 1850.

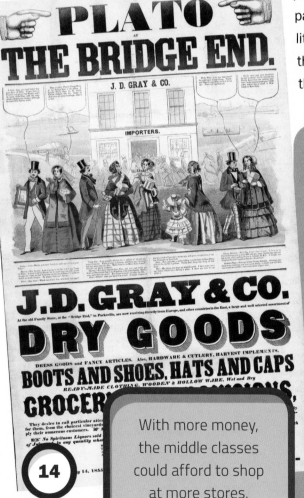

With more money, the middle classes could afford to shop at more stores.

14

25

Percentage of men in Philadelphia in 1860 who had middle-class jobs.

- The growth of cities and industry led to the rise of the middle classes during the Industrial Revolution.
- Jobs such as factory supervisors, accountants, and lawyers paid better than working-class jobs.
- The middle classes could afford to send their children to school for a better education.

GODEY'S MAGAZINE

FOR SEPTEMBER

TEN CENTS A COPY
ONE DOLLAR A YEAR

THE WOMAN THAT SAVED THE UNION

ANNA ELLA CARROLL, "Secret Member of Lincoln's Cabinet"

During the Industrial Revolution, the American middle classes grew larger and more prosperous.

Growing businesses and factories created many new jobs. Factories needed managers to watch over the workers. Businesses needed accountants and clerks. Growing cities needed more teachers, doctors, and lawyers. All of these people made up the middle classes.

People in the middle classes still had to work. But workers in the middle classes needed to have an education to do their jobs. They earned much more than laborers in factories and mills. They could afford better homes and better food. This allowed them to live longer and healthier lives. The middle classes could also afford new furniture and clothing. A child of the middle classes went to school instead of being sent to work. The middle classes enjoyed theater shows, concerts, and other leisure activities.

Middle-class women often did not work outside the home. Instead, they made managing their household and family their primary duties. They entertained guests in the parlor. They raised and oversaw the education of their children. They organized the family's social life.

Vanderbilt Builds a Railroad Empire

Cornelius Vanderbilt didn't start out rich. But as a young adult, he built steamships and operated a ferry in New York. By the time he was in his 60s, his company was one of the largest steamship operators in the United States.

In the 1860s, Vanderbilt turned his attention to railroads. The ongoing improvement of steam engines drove the construction of railroads. As the United States expanded into western territories, so too did the railroads. But many of the rail lines were short and owned by several different companies. They had different schedules. Even the tracks were different widths. It wasn't always easy to travel from one state to another. Vanderbilt saw an opportunity to create an empire. And he did not care if other people didn't like his methods.

Vanderbilt started buying up small rail lines. He combined them into a larger company and lowered his prices. Other companies couldn't afford to match those prices. They were forced to sell their businesses. Eventually, he owned a rail line from New York City to Chicago. Vanderbilt's rail lines all ran on the same schedule. This made transportation on his railroads more efficient and cheaper. Vanderbilt could again lower

Cornelius Vanderbilt

$100 million

Amount Cornelius Vanderbilt was worth when he died.

- The growth of western territories and new technology spurred the expansion of railroads.
- Vanderbilt bought small rail lines and combined them into a large corporation.
- He improved efficiency and lowered costs, which allowed him to build more rail lines.
- Vanderbilt was one of the richest people in the United States when he died.

CHINESE IMMIGRANTS WORK FOR RAILROADS

In 1865, Central Pacific was constructing part of the transcontinental railroad. Railroad work was hard. The company could not find enough white men who would stay. It opened up some jobs to Chinese immigrants. Although paid less, the Chinese immigrants performed some of the most difficult and dangerous tasks. By 1868, 12,000 Chinese immigrants worked for Central Pacific.

costs and build new rail lines. Other companies couldn't compete. Vanderbilt created one of the first giant corporations in the United States.

Although he started out poor, Vanderbilt did not give much of his money to charity. When he died in 1877, he left $1 million to start Vanderbilt University. That amounted to just 1 percent of his fortune.

Vanderbilt University in Nashville, Tennessee

The B&O Railroad Sells Stock

The rise of business during the Industrial Revolution led to the rise of stock exchanges in the United States. Stock exchanges allow companies to raise money by selling part of their ownership, or shares. During the Industrial Revolution, companies used this money to build new factories, railroads, telegraph lines, and more. Investors received a payment each year based on the company's profits, called a dividend.

In 1827, Philip Thomas wanted to build a railroad. He wanted it to stretch westward, from Baltimore, Maryland, to a city on the Ohio River. However, building a railroad was very expensive. He didn't have the $3 million it would cost to build it.

Thomas convinced several other businessmen to join him. They formed the Baltimore and Ohio Railroad Company. To raise the $3 million needed for the project, B&O offered 10,000 shares of stock to the State of Maryland and 5,000 shares to the City of Baltimore. Each share cost $100. They offered another

The B&O Railroad crossed the Potomac River.

15,000 shares to the public. People thought the new railroad was a good idea and quickly invested their money. All 15,000 shares of stock offered to the public sold out in only 12 days.

The company used the money raised in their stock sale to start building the railroad on July 4, 1828. But construction was slow and took many years. As each section of track was laid, the distance passengers and freight could travel grew. In December 1852, a B&O train finally reached Wheeling, West Virginia. It was the end of the line.

Investors did make money on the stocks they bought. But those looking to get rich quick were disappointed. The B&O made $3 million over the course of 17 years. But most of that money wasn't paid to investors. The company used the majority of the $3 million to keep building the railroad. Thomas did not make his fortune on the railroad either. He left the company in 1836.

8,500
Number of trades per day on the Stock Exchange in New York in 1835.

- Companies sold stocks to raise money for new factories, railroads, and telegraph lines.
- The Baltimore and Ohio Railroad Company offered shares of stock in 1827, and many people bought them.
- Started in 1828, the B&O finished its new railroad line in 1852.
- Investors saw little of B&O's profits early on.

Children Are Put to Work in Factories

During the Industrial Revolution, children were an important part of the workforce. Many poor children worked in factories or mines with a parent or sibling to help their families have enough money to live. Because they were small, children could fit into tight spaces and move quickly between factory machines. They were easy to control with threats. Children did not want to let their families down. Child workers were also paid much less than adults for the same work.

Working conditions for children were difficult and dangerous. Child workers often spent 10 to 14 hours per day at their jobs. They worked six days per week. They had few breaks. They also had to work near heavy and dangerous machinery. Many accidents injured or killed child workers. While at work, children were also exposed to fumes and toxins. Breathing in these chemicals damaged their lungs and made them sick. It also stunted their growth and development. Factory owners did not care. There were always more children who needed to work, ready

This boy worked in a mine in West Virginia.

President Woodrow Wilson signs a federal law limiting child labor in 1916.

to take another's place.

Children who worked in factories did not have time to attend school regularly. Without an education, many were unable to read or write. They couldn't gain the knowledge or skills needed to get better jobs.

Child workers were treated this way because the law allowed it. There were no federal laws restricting child labor. Eventually, some states passed laws that controlled child labor. These laws included a minimum working age and limited children's working hours. Unfortunately, these laws were rarely enforced. The federal government did not restrict child labor until 1916.

18

Percentage of industrial workers in the United States between the ages of 10 and 15 in 1890.

- Children went to work to help their families earn enough money to live.
- Children's jobs were often dangerous, but factory owners were not concerned about short-term or long-term effects.
- Working made it hard for children to go to school, so many couldn't read or write.
- There were no federal laws that protected child workers until 1916.

THINK ABOUT IT

How old do you think you should have to be to work in the United States today? Is the answer different if your family owns a business? What if your family really needs the money?

9

Labor Unions Fight for Worker Rights

In the 1800s, some workers were fed up. They were tired of working long days for little pay. Workers thought too many people were being injured on the job. They decided to do something about the poor working conditions in factories and mills. These workers formed a labor union. Labor unions bargained with factory owners for better wages, shorter workdays, and safer work environments. If union demands weren't met, workers refused to go to their jobs and went on strike. Sometimes these workers protested outside the company. They carried signs so other people would know about the strike. Labor unions also wanted companies to help workers who became sick or injured while on the job. They wanted to stop companies from using young children to do work.

The first labor unions were formed among people who did similar jobs, such as making shoes. But workers soon realized that a larger group made up of many unions could be even more powerful.

Members of the Ladies Tailor Union on strike in New York City

200,000

Number of workers in local labor unions across the United States in 1866.

- Labor unions formed to protect the rights of workers and to demand better pay and shorter workdays.
- The first unions were often made up of people who did similar jobs.
- Smaller unions joined together to create larger unions with more power.
- The NLU tried to protect workers' rights by asking Congress to pass federal laws.

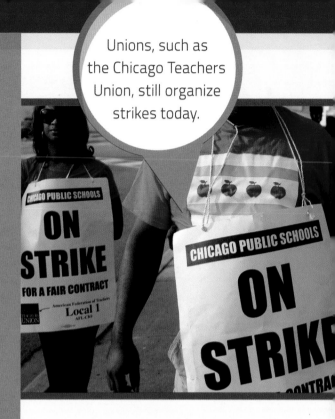

Unions, such as the Chicago Teachers Union, still organize strikes today.

In 1866, a group of labor unions joined together to form the National Labor Union (NLU).

THINK ABOUT IT

In 1981, President Ronald Reagan fired more than 12,000 air-traffic controllers who went on strike. Do a little research to find out how this changed labor unions. Is it illegal for some workers to strike?

The NLU did not want to bargain with individual owners and companies. The NLU did not think they would listen to its requests. Instead, the NLU wanted to change workers' rights through federal laws. The organization had limited success. In 1868, Congress passed a law limiting the workday to eight hours for federal employees. President Ulysses S. Grant said that employee wages would not be cut in response. This law was often ignored. But the NLU did make more people aware of labor issues. It opened the door for other labor organizations in the future.

Immigrants Come to the United States

Factories in the United States during the mid-1800s were growing. New inventions and innovations made it possible to make more products in a shorter amount of time. Factories needed more workers. Many people from other countries heard about jobs and land available in the United States. They decided to move to the United States, believing they could find a better life.

Millions of immigrants came from many different countries. They needed jobs as machines replaced their old skills. Most were trying to escape poverty. For example, in the 1840s and 1850s, many Irish immigrants arrived to escape a major famine in Ireland. These immigrants from Ireland and other countries settled in New York and other East Coast cities. They worked in coal mines, factories, and later in steel mills. Some came from German lands and traveled to the Midwest. Others came from China and worked to build railroads across the United States. Many immigrants moved to areas where people from their home countries already lived.

12 million

Number of immigrants that arrived in the United States between 1870 and 1900.

- Immigrants came to America to escape poverty and to find new work as their old jobs died out.
- Many employers took advantage of immigrants and paid them lower wages.
- Immigrants often faced discrimination at work and where they lived.

Many immigrants arrived in the United States with few possessions.

Employers soon realized the benefits of hiring immigrants. Immigrant workers rarely complained about poor working conditions. They were willing to do work that native-born Americans would not. Employers could get away with paying immigrants less than other workers. Immigrants also faced verbal and physical abuse while at work. Many immigrants continued working because they had to support their families.

Some immigrants experienced more discrimination than others. Those who had different religious beliefs, spoke a different language, or looked different than those with English ancestors were considered inferior. Chinese immigrants were treated especially poorly. Many native-born Americans saw them as unwanted competition for jobs. In 1882, Congress passed a federal law banning Chinese immigrants from coming to the United States.

Still, many immigrants continued to come to the United States looking for work. The large number of immigrants helped the United States become more diverse than ever before.

Andrew Carnegie's Philanthropy Is Criticized

Andrew Carnegie helped build the American steel industry. In 1901, Carnegie sold his businesses for $480 million. He became the richest man in the United States. But Carnegie's life started out much different. He was born in Scotland in 1835, and his parents were poor. His father lost his job and had to beg for

work. His mother mended shoes to help support the family. Carnegie's mother had to borrow money so his family could move to the United States. As a young boy, Carnegie was determined to cure poverty.

After selling his company, Carnegie wanted to use his fortune to help

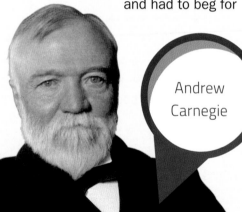

Andrew Carnegie

CARNEGIE'S STEEL

On a trip to Europe, Carnegie learned about a new method for making steel from iron. Carnegie brought the idea back to the United States. He built a new steel plant near Pittsburgh, Pennsylvania. At the same time, Carnegie was careful to keep costs low. He bought other steel plants. By 1900, he controlled approximately 25 percent of the country's steel industry.

2,500
Public libraries established by Andrew Carnegie.

- Carnegie was born in Scotland and grew up poor.
- He made a fortune in the steel industry, but Carnegie wanted to give away his money after he retired.
- Carnegie created libraries and other organizations to help people, but some criticized his philanthropy.

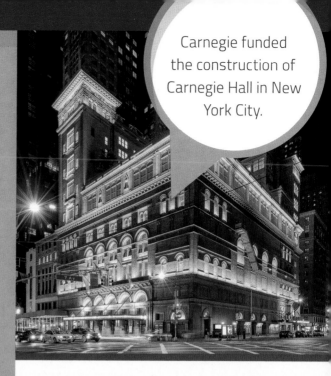

Carnegie funded the construction of Carnegie Hall in New York City.

others. He donated more than $43 million to establish thousands of libraries. He supported many colleges, schools, and other organizations. He believed these groups would help people gain new skills so they could make more money. He formed the Carnegie Corporation of New York to give away more of his money. By the time he died in 1919, Carnegie had given away approximately $350 million.

Not everyone supported Carnegie's philanthropy efforts. Many people criticized him. Some said he became rich only by paying workers low wages. Others accused him of trying to use his money to gain influence over universities and their scientific research. The criticism frustrated Carnegie. Carnegie also did not give away money directly to people who were poor. He thought people of the working class would spend any extra money on alcohol.

Many of the libraries and organizations Carnegie started are still around more than 100 years later. The Carnegie Institution of Washington continues to fund scientific research. The institution has helped scientists discover more about DNA and the universe.

12

Henry Ford Doubles Worker Pay

In 1908, Henry Ford and the Ford Motor Company introduced the Model T car. Ford wanted to make an automobile that average Americans could afford. Ford searched for ways to increase production and lower costs. He began experimenting with the moving assembly line. By 1913, the Ford Motor Company was producing thousands of cars every week.

Assembly line workers hated the jobs. They stood in one place and repeated the same task over and over again. Many quit working in Ford's factory

a few days or weeks after they were hired. Constantly hiring new workers was expensive. It cost time and money to train them. Sometimes workers simply walked away from the assembly line. This caused production to come to a standstill. Ford realized he needed a way to make workers want to stay in his factory.

On January 5, 1914, Ford's company announced that it would double workers' pay. It also shortened the workday. Before, workers earned $2.34 for nine hours of work. Now most would earn $5.00 for only eight hours. Other company owners

Assembly line for the Model T in 1913

28

said Ford was crazy. They said it was too expensive. Ford didn't raise wages out of charity, though. He did it to stabilize his workforce. In exchange for $5.00 per day, workers were watched closely, sometimes even in their own homes. They were expected to avoid drinking and gambling, and immigrants had to learn English. Workers who didn't follow these rules received less pay. But thousands of people applied for a job at Ford's plant. And workers could now afford the cars they were building. With fewer people quitting, Ford's assembly lines were able to produce more cars at a low cost.

HOW THE ASSEMBLY LINE WORKS

On Ford's assembly line, a conveyor belt carried parts past a line of workers. Each worker stood in one spot. The worker added one piece to the automobile. Then the conveyor belt moved the car onward to another worker. The assembly line was very efficient. Before the assembly line, workers needed 12 hours to build a complete car. The assembly line made it possible to complete a car in only 1.5 hours.

10,000
Number of people who came to Ford's Highland Park Plant looking for a job on January 6, 1914.

- Ford used the moving assembly line to build cars efficiently.
- Workers disliked doing the same job over and over, so many quit.
- Ford's company doubled workers' pay to get them to stay on the job.
- The changes made it possible to produce more cars in a shorter amount of time.

Glossary

competition
A person or group trying to succeed against others to get the same thing.

efficient
Taking as little time as possible.

gin
A slang term for an engine, a tool, or a mechanical device.

immigrants
People who move to a foreign country to live.

investors
People who put money into a company and expect to be paid back more in the future.

labor union
A group of workers that bargains with an employer.

privilege
Advantages or special rights given to a certain person or group of people.

slums
Run-down and crowded places to live, usually in a city.

strike
When workers walk off the job and refuse to return to work until their demands are met.

textile
Cloth or fabric.

toxic
Poisonous.

working class
People who work in factories, in mines, on farms, or at other jobs using their hands.

For More Information

Books

Garstecki, Julia. *Life during the Industrial Revolution*. Minneapolis: Abdo, 2015.

Mullenback, Cheryl. *The Industrial Revolution for Kids: The People and Technology That Changed the World, with 21 Activities*. Chicago: Chicago Review Press, 2014.

Niver, Heather Moore. *Eli Whitney and the Industrial Revolution*. New York: PowerKids Press, 2017.

Visit 12StoryLibrary.com

Scan the code or use your school's login at **12StoryLibrary.com** for recent updates about this topic and a full digital version of this book. Enjoy free access to:

- Digital ebook
- Breaking news updates
- Live content feeds
- Videos, interactive maps, and graphics
- Additional web resources

Note to educators: Visit 12StoryLibrary.com/register to sign up for free premium website access. Enjoy live content plus a full digital version of every 12-Story Library book you own for every student at your school.

Index

About the Author

Carla Mooney is the author of many books for young readers. She loves investigating science and history and learning about new perspectives. A graduate of the University of Pennsylvania, Mooney lives in Pittsburgh with her husband and children.

READ MORE FROM 12-STORY LIBRARY

Every 12-Story Library book is available in many formats. For more information, visit 12StoryLibrary.com.